1 MONTH OF
FREE
READING

at
www.ForgottenBooks.com

By purchasing this book you are eligible for one month membership to ForgottenBooks.com, giving you unlimited access to our entire collection of over 1,000,000 titles via our web site and mobile apps.

To claim your free month visit: www.forgottenbooks.com/free896393

ISBN 978-0-265-83422-0
PIBN 10896393

Essentials
of
An Adequate
Diet

...facts for nutrition programs

Home Economics Research Report No.

Agricultural Research Service
United States Department of Agriculture

About this publication

Food supplies available in this country are sufficient in variety and amount to furnish every individual with the nutrients recommended for good nutrition. However, surveys show that many people could improve their diets, particularly in calcium and vitamins A and C, by wiser food selection. It is evident that there is a continuing need for sound information as a basis for teaching the average individual to choose foods intelligently.

Essentials of an Adequate Diet is designed as source material for nutritionists, extension workers, and others who are teaching the principles of good food selection. The aim has been to provide enough basic facts about food values to promote flexibility in food choices with reasonable assurance that a good diet will be obtained day by day, week by week. Many workers no doubt will wish to adapt this material to their own teaching needs. For example, some may wish to use the information on food sources of vitamins to strengthen their use of other food guides.

The basic scheme given here—A Daily Food Plan—was developed in response to many requests for up-to-date material to use in nutrition education programs. This does not mean that other food guides or teaching devices are no longer useful. There are many possible ways of presenting the essentials of an adequate diet. Some are suitable for one purpose, some for another.

Many nutrition workers will wish to know how reliable the daily food plan is in providing an adequate diet. Partial answers to this question are given in the last section. Included in this section also is a discussion of the use and limitations of food plans for appraising diet records.

Essentials of an Adequate Diet is the first of a series, Facts for Nutrition Programs, being developed as reference for nutrition workers. This bulletin is a slight revision of and supersedes AIB-160, issued under the same title in November 1956.

This publication was prepared by Louise Page and Esther F. Phipard, Institute of Home Economics, Agricultural Research Service.

Acknowledgment is made of suggestions and guidance received from many reviewers, especially the members of the Interagency Committee on Nutrition Education and School Lunch.

Issued November 1957

Essentials of an Adequate Diet

. . . facts for nutrition programs

A daily food plan

For health our daily food must supply many kinds of nutrients—proteins, minerals, vitamins, fats, carbohydrates. Most foods contain more than one nutrient, but no single food furnishes all the necessary nutrients in proper proportions to maintain good health. It is not difficult to obtain the nutrients needed if the types of foods listed below are eaten daily in the amounts suggested.

Milk group: Some milk daily—

Children.	3 to 4 cups.
Teen-agers.	4 or more cups.
Adults.	2 or more cups.
Pregnant women.	4 or more cups.
Nursing mothers.	6 or more cups.

Cheese and ice cream can replace part of the milk. (See p. 4)

Meat group: 2 or more servings—

Beef, veal, pork, lamb, poultry, fish, eggs, with dry beans and peas and nuts as alternates.

Vegetable-fruit group: 4 or more servings, including—

A dark-green or deep-yellow vegetable important for vitamin A—at least every other day.

A citrus fruit or other fruit or vegetable important for vitamin C—daily.

Other fruits and vegetables including potatoes.

Bread-cereals group: 4 or more servings—

Whole grain, enriched, restored.

The minimum number of servings listed above forms a *foundation* for a good diet. To round out meals and to satisfy the appetite many people will use more of these foods and everyone will use foods not specified—butter, margarine, other fats, oils, sugars, and unenriched refined grain products. These "other" foods are frequently combined with the suggested foods in mixed dishes, baked goods, desserts, and other recipe dishes. Fats, oils, and sugars are also added to many foods during preparation and at the table to enhance flavor and improve appetite appeal. Thus these foods are a part of daily meals, even though they are not stressed in the food plan.

Importance of the food groups

Each of the broad food groups listed in the daily food plan has a special job to do in helping toward an adequate diet. In the number of servings specified and with the choices indicated, these food groups together furnish all or a major share of the calcium, protein, iron, vitamins A and C, and the B-vitamins recommended by nutritionists (chart 1). These foods also provide other vitamins and minerals as well as fats and carbohydrates important for good nutrition.

Experience shows that with the patterns of eating in this country, the additional foods used will bring the calorie level up to or beyond 100 percent. Whether or not other dietary needs are met depends on choices made within food groups and also on the kinds of foods selected to provide the remaining calories.

Choices within food groups.—Each of the food groups, with the exception of bread and cereals, is counted on to furnish a large part of the daily allowance for one or more key nutrients. The milk group is counted on for calcium; the meat group for protein; certain vegetables and fruits for vitamin A—others for vitamin C. The material that follows is intended to show how to get the amount of calcium expected from the milk group, the amount of protein from the meat group, and so on.

Chart 1

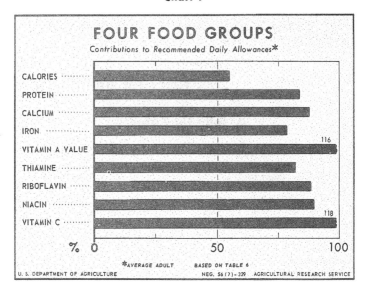

FOUR FOOD GROUPS
Contributions to Recommended Daily Allowances*

CALORIES

PROTEIN

CALCIUM

IRON

VITAMIN A VALUE 116

THIAMINE

RIBOFLAVIN

NIACIN 118

VITAMIN C

% 0 50 100

*AVERAGE ADULT   BASED ON TABLE 6

U. S. DEPARTMENT OF AGRICULTURE   NEG. 56 (7)-329   AGRICULTURAL RESEARCH SERVICE

Although foods within each group are much alike in food value, they vary in the amounts of nutrients provided by a serving. To help in making choices, foods in each group have been rated in points to show how they compare as sources of a key nutrient. For each nutrient, 20 points represents the minimum counted on from a particular food group and corresponds to nearly half or more of the day's allowance for an average adult.[1] Most or all of the remainder needed to give recommended amounts will be furnished anyway by the other food groups; thus there is no need to count up the total daily intake.

This point system provides a way to check daily food choices to make sure that the food group as a whole furnishes the amount of a key nutrient expected of it. It has the added advantages of dealing with simple whole numbers, and of employing the same term—"point"— for each nutrient. For those who prefer to

[1]See footnote 5, table 6.

make calculations in conventional units, nutrient values in grams, milligrams, and International Units are also shown.

Because the point values of foods are based on allowances for an average adult, adjustments will be necessary for checking food selections of children, teen-agers, and pregnant and nursing women. As a general rule, except for milk, young children need less of all foods than adults; older children need about the same amounts as adults. Teen-agers, active adults, and pregnant and nursing women require more of most kinds of foods.

The kinds and quantities of foods that furnish desirable amounts of these four key nutrients, plus the suggested servings from the bread-cereals group, will also supply a large share of the needs for other nutrients with the possible exception of calories (chart 1). For this reason it is not necessary to check food selections for amounts of each nutrient supplied.

Milk group
Milk, cheese, ice cream

Milk is a leading source of calcium, essential for the development of bones and teeth and required for the proper functioning of muscles and nerves and for the normal clotting of blood. In addition, milk is an important contributor of riboflavin and high-quality protein and also provides many other vitamins and minerals, as well as carbohydrates and fats. Cheese and ice cream supply these nutrients, too, but in different proportions.

Chart 2 shows the nutrients supplied by 2 cups of milk, the minimum quantity specified for adults, and how this quantity helps meet the daily allowances for an average adult.

Because of its importance as a source of calcium, milk is counted on to furnish the major portion of the daily needs for this mineral. The minimum amounts of milk specified provide over two-thirds of the calcium recommended for a day. Foods from other groups, chiefly vegetables, fruits, breads, and cereals, in the amount suggested in this guide, will supply the remainder.

On the basis of calcium content, cheese and ice cream can be used to replace part of the milk recommended for a day. Table 1 shows how common milk products compare as sources of calcium. In rating these foods, 20 calcium points correspond to about 600 milligrams of calcium. This is equivalent to the calcium contained in 2 cups of milk and is the minimum counted on each day from this group for adults.

Either calcium points or actual values in milligrams can be used in checking food selections to make sure that the amount of calcium expected from the milk group is supplied. The following combinations show different ways of

Chart 2

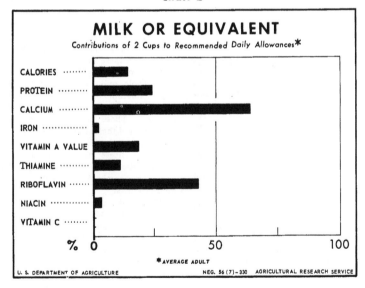

MILK OR EQUIVALENT

Contributions of 2 Cups to Recommended Daily Allowances*

CALORIES
PROTEIN
CALCIUM
IRON
VITAMIN A VALUE
THIAMINE
RIBOFLAVIN
NIACIN
VITAMIN C

% 0   50   100

*AVERAGE ADULT

U. S. DEPARTMENT OF AGRICULTURE   NEG. 56 (7)–330   AGRICULTURAL RESEARCH SERVICE

Table 1.—*Common milk products as sources of calcium*

Food	Amount	Calcium	
		Points [1]	Milligrams
Milk:			
Whole, fluid...........................	1 cup....................	10	290
Skim, fluid...........................	1 cup...................	10	300
Buttermilk...........................	1 cup...................	10	290
Whole, dry...........................	3 to 4 tablespoons..............	9	260
Nonfat, dry...........................	3 to 4 tablespoons...............	11	340
Evaporated, undiluted.................	½ cup...................	10	310
Cheese:			
Cottage...........................	¼ cup...................	2	50
Cream...........................	¼ cup...................	1	40
Natural or processed, such as cheddar or swiss......	1 ounce...................	7	190
Ice cream...........................	½ cup...................	3	90
Sherbet, milk...........................	½ cup...................	2	50

[1] One calcium point is equivalent to about 30 milligrams of calcium.

obtaining at least 20 calcium points—or about 600 milligrams of calcium.

	Calcium	
	Points	Milli-grams
½ cup cottage cheese...............	4	100
1½ cups skim milk.................	15	450
½ cup milk sherbet.................	2	50
	21	600
½ cup evaporated milk.............	10	310
1 ounce cheddar cheese.............	7	190
½ cup ice cream...................	3	90
	20	590
3 to 4 tablespoons nonfat dry milk.....	11	340
1 cup buttermilk...................	10	290
	21	630

Milk is of special value for at least two nutrients in addition to calcium—protein and riboflavin. The protein of milk is of high quality. It is efficient when used alone because all the amino acids essential for human growth and development are present in favorable proportions, and it supplements the protein of bread and other grain products when used with them. The minimum amounts of milk suggested provide about one-fourth the protein and nearly half the riboflavin recommended for adults, while for children the milk quota supplies as much as half the needed protein and over half the riboflavin. Cheese and ice cream also furnish these two nutrients.

Whole milk, evaporated milk, cheese made from whole milk, and ice cream contribute appreciable amounts of vitamin A, dependent upon the concentration of butterfat in the product. Those forms of milk from which most or all of the butterfat has been removed—such as skim milk, buttermilk, nonfat dry milk, and cheese made from skim milk—contribute little of this vitamin except when fortified with vitamin A concentrate, as are some fluid products.

Whole milk normally contains small amounts of vitamin D. Milk to which vitamin D has been added becomes a valuable source of this nutrient. A quart of vitamin D milk provides the recommended daily allowance for vitamin D for children.

When fluid milk, or its equivalent in other forms, is omitted from the day's meals or used only in small amounts, calcium, and sometimes riboflavin, is likely to fall below amounts recommended for good nutrition.

4

Meat group
Meat, fish, poultry, eggs, dry beans and peas, nuts

The foods of the meat group are important for the amounts and quality of the protein they provide. Protein is important mainly as a tissue builder. This nutrient is a vital part of muscle, organs, blood, skin, hair, and other living tissue. Besides protein, many of these foods supply considerable iron, thiamine, riboflavin, and niacin. They also furnish other minerals and vitamins and variable quantities of fat.

Chart 3 shows the nutrients provided by two servings of foods from the meat group and how they help meet the daily allowances for an average adult. Although some foods in this group have more of a nutrient, and some less, the group is likely to average as shown.

In this food plan, foods from the meat group are relied on to contribute about half the protein recommended for a day. The rest will come from foods of the other groups primarily from milk, breads, and cereals.

Table 2 shows how different foods of this group compare as sources of protein. These foods are rated in points on the basis of how well they supply the protein equivalent of 4 ounces of lean cooked meat without bone—2 small servings. This amount of protein, about 30 grams, is assigned a point value of 20 and is the minimum counted on each day from this group for adults.

Foods from this table are needed each day in amounts to furnish at least 20 protein points, or about 30 grams of protein, the share counted on from the meat group. Combinations of these foods can be used. For example:

	Protein Points	Grams
2 ounces beef.....................	10	15
1 egg............................	4	6
½ cup cooked navy beans..........	6	8
	20	29
2 ounces fish......................	10	15
2 ounces pork.....................	10	15
	20	30

Chart 3

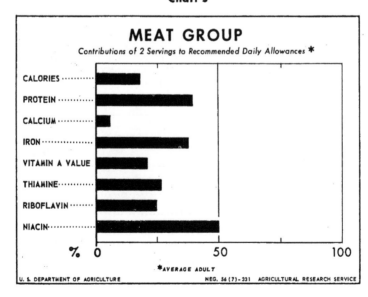

MEAT GROUP

Contributions of 2 Servings to Recommended Daily Allowances *

CALORIES
PROTEIN
CALCIUM
IRON
VITAMIN A VALUE
THIAMINE
RIBOFLAVIN
NIACIN

%   0   50   100

*AVERAGE ADULT

U. S. DEPARTMENT OF AGRICULTURE   NEG. 56(7)-331   AGRICULTURAL RESEARCH SERVICE

| | Protein | |
	Points	Grams
2 eggs.........................	8	12
4 slices bacon.................	6	8
2 tablespoons peanut butter.........	6	8
	20	28
3 ounces veal..................	15	22
2 ounces bologna..............	6	9
	21	31
3 ounces poultry..............	15	22
2 ounces luncheon meat...........	6	9
	21	31

Cheese and milk are also good sources of high-quality protein and, in the amounts specified for calcium in the milk group, are already depended on to furnish an important share of the protein allowance. If more is used than is needed for calcium, the extra milk and cheese can count toward the 20 protein points suggested from the meat group. Protein values for milk and cheese are as follows:

| | | Protein | |
	Amount	Points	Grams
Milk, whole, fluid....	1 cup........	6	8
Cheese:			
Cheddar..........	1 ounce.....	5	7
Cottage...........	¼ cup......	7	11
Cream...........	¼ cup......	3	5

Some meat, fish, eggs, milk, or cheese at each meal is recommended for effective use of protein in the diet. The high-quality protein furnished by the animal foods of the meat group—meat, poultry, fish, eggs—is of special importance to good nutrition because it contains all of the essential amino acids in the proportions needed to support growth and to maintain health. The other foods of this group—dry beans and peas and nuts—also supply considerable protein but it is of a lower quality; that is, one or more of the essential amino acids occur in unfavorable proportions. However, the value of these foods as protein contributors is increased when they are supplemented in the same meal with high-quality protein, such as that from the animal sources already listed or from milk.

The meat group as a whole is also valuable for iron, thiamine, riboflavin, and niacin. It is depended on to provide about half the iron recommended daily. Important sources of this mineral include lean meats, variety meats such as liver, heart, and kidney, egg yolk, and dry beans.

Thiamine is widely distributed in foods, but there are very few rich sources of this nutrient; the lean meat of pork is one of the richest. One or two servings each week of lean pork—fresh or cured—will help to assure recommended amounts of thiamine. Other protein foods that furnish considerable thiamine are dry beans and peas and variety meats.

Of the meat group, variety meats are high in riboflavin. Leading providers of niacin include lean meats, variety meats, fish, poultry, peanuts, and peanut butter.

Table 2.—Foods of the meat group as sources of protein

| Food | Amount | Protein | |
		Points [1]	Grams
Beef, veal, lamb, pork, poultry—lean, cooked, without bone...	2 ounces...........................	10	15
Bacon..	2 slices.............................	3	4
Dry beans and peas, cooked...........................	½ cup.............................	6	8
Eggs...	1 egg..............................	4	6
Fish, cooked, without bone..........................	2 ounces...........................	10	15
Frankfurters	2 ounces...........................	6	8
Luncheon meat..	2 ounces...........................	6	9
Peanut butter...	2 tablespoons......................	6	8

[1] One protein point is equivalent to about 1.5 grams of protein. Because both points and grams are rounded to whole numbers, the equivalent is 1.3 for some items.

Vegetable-fruit group

Vegetables and fruits are valuable because of the vitamins and minerals they contain, as well as for the interest they add to meals and for the roughage they provide.

Dark-green and deep-yellow vegetables are noteworthy for vitamin A, necessary for normal growth and development in children and for general health of adults. This vitamin is needed for healthy skin, including the inner linings of the body, and also influences the ability of the eye to adjust to limited amounts of light. Many dark-green vegetables also provide worthwhile quantities of vitamin C, iron, riboflavin, and calcium.

Citrus fruits are a leading source of ascorbic acid (vitamin C), which is a vital part of the material that helps to hold body cells together and therefore is of importance to healthy growth and maintenance of teeth, bone, tissues, and blood vessels.

Chart 4 shows the nutrients provided by four servings of vegetables and fruits—including the specified servings of citrus fruits, dark-green or deep-yellow vegetables, and other vegetables and fruits—and how they help meet the daily allowances for an average adult.

Although fruits and vegetables in each of these classifications make similar nutrient contributions, they vary in the amounts of nutrients furnished by a serving; the values shown are averages.

Vegetables and fruits are rated in tables 3 and 4 as sources of vitamin A value and vitamin C, respectively. In general, the foods compared are common to all sections of this country. Other vegetables and fruits used locally that are noteworthy for either of these nutrients can be rated in a similar manner and added to the lists.

Dark-green and deep-yellow vegetables for vitamin A

Dark-green and deep-yellow vegetables and other vegetables and fruits important for vitamin A are depended on in this food plan to provide for at least half the recommended amount of this nutrient. The remainder will come chiefly from the servings of other fruits and vegetables suggested in the daily plan and from whole milk, cheese, ice cream, butter or margarine, eggs, and the occasional use of liver.

Although vitamin A, as such, does not occur in vegetables and fruits, these foods contain carotene which is changed by the body to

Chart 4

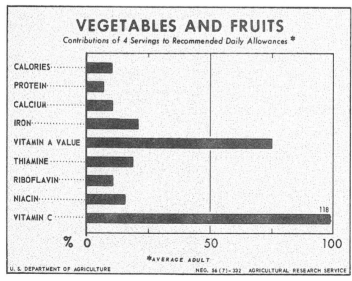

VEGETABLES AND FRUITS
Contributions of 4 Servings to Recommended Daily Allowances *

CALORIES
PROTEIN
CALCIUM
IRON
VITAMIN A VALUE
THIAMINE
RIBOFLAVIN
NIACIN
VITAMIN C ... 118

% 0 ... 50 ... 100

*AVERAGE ADULT

U. S. DEPARTMENT OF AGRICULTURE   NEG. 56 (7)-332   AGRICULTURAL RESEARCH SERVICE

Table 3.—Vegetables and fruits as sources of vitamin A value

Food	Amount	Vitamin A Points [1]	Vitamin A I. U.
Beet greens	½ cup	45	5,400
Broccoli	½ cup	20	2,500
Carrots, diced	½ cup	70	9,050
Chard, leaves	½ cup	70	8,500
Collards	½ cup	60	7,250
Cress, garden	½ cup	25	2,950
Dandelion greens	½ cup	110	13,650
Kale	½ cup	35	4,600
Mustard greens	½ cup	40	5,000
Peppers, sweet, red, raw	½ medium	15	1,800
Pumpkin	½ cup	30	3,850
Spinach	½ cup	75	9,100
Squash, winter, yellow	½ cup	50	6,000
Sweetpotatoes, yellow	½ medium	40	5,200
Tomatoes, cooked or juice	½ cup	10	1,250
Tomatoes, raw	1 medium	15	1,650
Turnip greens	½ cup	60	7,700
Apricots, raw or cooked	5 halves	20	2,300
Cantaloup	½ medium	50	6,200

[1] One vitamin A point is equivalent to about 125 I. U. of vitamin A.

vitamin A. In table 3, important vegetable and fruit sources of carotene are compared as providers of vitamin A value. In rating these foods in points, 2,500 International Units of vitamin A is used as the baseline and corresponds to 20 vitamin A points.

The measures given in the table are for raw fruits and for cooked vegetables unless otherwise indicated. If used raw instead of cooked, the vegetables also contribute considerable vitamin A value. However, the amount furnished by a half-cup portion will usually be less, primarily because of difference in weight.

A daily serving from the foods listed is not necessary because several of them supply much more vitamin A value than is needed for a day, and the body can store large amounts of this nutrient. However, to assure the share of this vitamin counted on from dark-green and yellow vegetables and other vegetables and fruits high in carotene, foods from this group must provide at least 140 vitamin A points *a week*— equivalent to 20 points a day. This corresponds to at least 17,500 I. U. of vitamin A value a week or an average of 2,500 I. U. a day.

Depending on choices, a serving of these foods at least every other day can provide 140 or more vitamin A points or at least 17,500 I. U. of vitamin A value—the amount counted on from this group each week. For example:

	Vitamin A Points	I. U.
½ cup broccoli	20	2,550
5 halves canned apricots	20	2,300
½ cup carrots	70	9,050
½ medium sweetpotato (yellow)	40	5,200
	150	19,100
½ medium cantaloup	50	6,200
½ cup spinach	75	9,100
½ cup tomato juice	10	1,250
½ cup winter squash (yellow)	50	6,000
	185	22,550
½ cup chard	70	8,500
½ cup carrots	70	9,050
1 medium tomato	15	1,650
½ cup beet greens	45	5,400
	200	24,600

	Vitamin A	
	Points	I. U.
½ cup kale........................	35	4,600
1 medium sweetpotato (yellow).......	80	10,400
½ cup tomato juice.................	10	1,250
½ cup broccoli....................	20	2,550
	145	18,800

Even though it is possible to get the share of vitamin A expected from this group each week from only 2 servings of some of the listed foods, fewer servings than 1 every other day are not recommended because these foods are also relied on to furnish other nutrients besides vitamin A. For instance, many dark-green leafy vegetables furnish appreciable amounts of vitamin C, calcium, iron, and riboflavin.

There is no need to restrict the size of servings to those shown, but in using this list—or the others given—it is important to stress that larger or smaller servings furnish more or less of a nutrient and to adjust points accordingly.

Another fact to emphasize is that the number of points, or level of a particular nutrient, counted on from a food group is the minimum; more would be desirable.

Citrus fruits and other fruits and vegetables high in vitamin C

Citrus fruits and other fruits and vegetables high in ascorbic acid are relied on in this food plan to contribute at least two-thirds of the daily recommended allowances for this nutrient. The remainder will come primarily from the specified servings of other fruits and vegetables.

Important vegetable and fruit sources of vitamin C are compared in table 4 as contributors of this nutrient. In rating these foods, 50 milligrams of ascorbic acid, the minimum amount expected to come from this group each day, corresponds to 20 vitamin C points.

The amounts shown in the table for citrus fruits are for the fresh, canned, or frozen item; the quantities given for other fruits are for raw fruits. The vegetables are cooked unless other-

Table 4.—Fruits and vegetables as sources of vitamin C

Food	Amount	Vitamin C	
		Points [1]	Milligrams
Grapefruit...	½ medium...........................	30	76
Grapefruit juice......................................	½ cup.............................	17	43
Orange..	1 medium..........................	31	77
Orange juice...	½ cup.............................	19	48
Tangerine..	1 medium..........................	10	25
Tangerine juice.......................................	½ cup.............................	13	32
Cantaloup...	½ medium..........................	24	59
Honeydew melon......................................	1 wedge, 2 by 7 inches...............	14	34
Pineapple, fresh, diced................................	½ cup.............................	6	16
Strawberries...	½ cup.............................	18	44
Broccoli...	½ cup.............................	22	56
Brussels sprouts......................................	½ cup.............................	12	30
Cabbage, raw, shredded...............................	½ cup.............................	10	25
Greens:			
Collards, mustard greens, turnip greens.............	½ cup.............................	13	32
Garden cress, kale...............................	½ cup.............................	10	26
Spinach...	½ cup.............................	9	22
Peppers, green, raw or cooked..........................	1 small............................	17	43
Peppers, sweet, red, raw...............................	½ medium..........................	31	78
Potato, cooked in jacket...............................	1 medium..........................	8	20
Sweetpotato, boiled or baked...........................	1 medium..........................	10	26
Tomatoes, cooked or juice.............................	½ cup.............................	8	19
Tomato, raw...	1 medium..........................	14	35

[1] One vitamin C point is equivalent to about 2 or 3 milligrams of ascorbic acid.

9

wise indicated. When used raw the vegetables listed as cooked also provide valuable amounts of ascorbic acid; moreover, the amounts supplied are usually higher than those shown for the cooked food.

A single food or a combination of the listed foods can be used to provide a total of at least 20 vitamin C points daily—equivalent to about 50 milligrams of ascorbic acid—the amount counted on in this plan from vitamin C-rich foods. For example:

	Vitamin C Points	Milligrams
1 medium orange..................	31	77
½ cup broccoli.....................	22	56
½ medium cantaloup................	24	59
1 small green pepper, cooked........	17	43
1 medium potato, cooked in jacket. ...	8	20
	25	63
½ cup tomato juice.................	8	19
½ cup brussels sprouts..............	12	30
	20	49
1 medium baked sweetpotato.........	10	26
½ cup kale........................	10	26
	20	52

Sources of both vitamin A value and vitamin C

Several vegetables and fruits are valuable sources of both vitamin A value and vitamin C. For example, the tables of important sources of both these nutrients include broccoli, kale, spinach, and other greens, sweet red peppers, sweetpotatoes, tomatoes, and cantaloup. A serving of any of these foods counts toward both the vitamin A and vitamin C quota. For instance:

	Vitamin A Points	I. U.		Vitamin C Points	Mg.
½ cup broccoli.........	20	2,550	and	22	56
½ medium cantaloup....	50	6,200	and	24	59
½ cup tomato juice......	10	1,250	and	8	19

However, if a serving is counted as a source of both vitamin A and vitamin C, at least 3 other servings from the vegetable-fruit group are still needed to make up the specified 4 or more daily servings from this group.

Other fruits and vegetables including potatoes

Other common fruits and vegetables not specified as sources of either vitamin A or C do not rate high enough in these nutrients to be included in table 3 or 4. However, they are useful and can be counted to reach the recommended four servings because their smaller amounts of nutrients help to add up to an adequate diet.

Potatoes are used almost daily by most people in this country because of their availability, low cost, and general acceptance. In the quantities used they are valuable for many nutrients including iron, thiamine, and niacin. When cooked in the jacket to conserve nutrients, potatoes also furnish enough vitamin C to be included in the list of sources of this vitamin.

Bread-cereals group

Breads and cereals—whole grain, enriched, restored—furnish worthwhile amounts of thiamine, protein, iron, and niacin, and also help out with other vitamins and minerals and with food energy. Chart 5 shows the nutrients provided by four servings from this food group, and how they help meet the daily allowances for an average adult.

The importance of grain foods in the diet rests on their many-sided nutritional contribution at relatively low cost rather than on large contributions of one or two nutrients. For this reason foods of this group are not rated as sources of a specific nutrient.

The bread–cereals group includes any of the following foods if they are *whole grain, enriched, restored* (check the labels to be sure): Bread, cooked cereals, ready-to-eat cereals, cornmeal, crackers, flour, grits, macaroni, noodles, rice, rolled oats, and spaghetti. Biscuits, muffins, cake, cookies, and other baked goods made with whole grain or enriched flour can also be counted.

In developing the daily food plan, 4 servings from this group were figured as 3 slices of bread and 1 serving of cereal (1 ounce of ready-to-eat cereal or ½ to ¾ cup of cooked cereal including rice, cornmeal, grits, macaroni, etc.). If none of these cereals are eaten, 2 slices of bread can be used instead, making a total of 5 slices for the day.

Chart 5

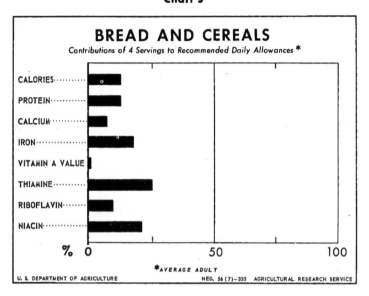

BREAD AND CEREALS

Contributions of 4 Servings to Recommended Daily Allowances *

CALORIES··········

PROTEIN··········

CALCIUM··········

IRON··············

VITAMIN A VALUE

THIAMINE··········

RIBOFLAVIN·······

NIACIN··········

% 0   50   100

*AVERAGE ADULT

U. S. DEPARTMENT OF AGRICULTURE   NEG. 56(7)-333   AGRICULTURAL RESEARCH SERVICE

Cereal protein is relatively low in some of the amino acids necessary for good nutrition. It is used more effectively by the body when eaten in the same meal with proteins from other foods, such as milk, meat, fish, poultry, and eggs.

The amount of calcium provided by this group of foods depends to a large extent on the ingredients of bread. The use of milk, milk solids, and calcium-containing mold inhibitors, dough conditioners, and yeast foods adds in varying amounts to the calcium content of bread.

Enrichment of cereal foods with iron, thiamine, riboflavin, and niacin accounts for appreciable amounts of these nutrients in the average diet. Whole grain and enriched cereal products are especially important because they are reliable sources of thiamine and there are only a few foods high in this vitamin.

Unenriched refined cereal foods can be used, in addition to the specified servings of whole grain or enriched bread and cereals, to add variety to meals and to provide extra food energy, if needed.

To complete the diet

The foods suggested in this guide provide a *foundation* for an adequate diet. The minimum number of servings specified from each food group together provide most, but not all, of the nutrients needed for good nutrition. A glance at chart 1 shows which nutrients are likely to be short unless additional or extra-large servings of foods listed in the daily plan are used, along with other foods not emphasized.

Sources of nutrients not already stressed in the food plan are discussed below to guide in making additional choices from food groups.

Calories.—Depending on choices from the four food groups, about one-third to one-half of the calorie allowance for an average adult still needs to be supplied. Many people will use more than the minimum number of servings specified in the guide, as well as butter, margarine, other fats, unenriched refined cereal products, sugars, and sweets, to round out meals and to provide additional calories as needed.

11

The following list shows the calorie values for a few selected foods:

	Amount	Calories
Apple................	1 medium..............	75
Bacon.................	1 slice..................	50
Banana................	1 medium..............	90
Bread.................	1 slice..................	65
Butter or margarine......	1 teaspoon.............	35
Cake, iced.............	1 piece, 3 by 2 by 1½ inches.	290
Carrots, cooked.........	½ cup................	20
Cheese, cheddar.........	1 ounce...............	115
Eggs..................	1 egg..................	75
Hamburger, cooked.....	3 ounces..............	315
Lettuce................	1 large leaf............	5
Luncheon meat.........	1 slice.................	85
Milk, skim.............	1 cup..................	85
Milk, whole............	1 cup..................	165
Oatmeal, cooked.......	½ cup.................	75
Orange juice...........	½ cup.................	55
Pie, two crust..........	4-inch sector (9-inch diameter).	325
Pork chop.............	1 medium..............	295
Potato.................	1 medium..............	100
Salad dressing.........	1 tablespoon...........	60
Sugar, sirup, jam.......	1 tablespoon...........	60
Tomato................	1 medium..............	30

Iron.—On an average almost four-fifths of the iron allowance for an adult is provided by the foods specified in the daily plan. Except for milk, each of the food groups contributes worthwhile amounts of iron. For instance, the meat group furnishes about half the daily allowance; the vegetable and fruit group, about a fourth—chiefly from the dark-green leafy vegetables; and whole grain, enriched, or restored cereal foods in the minimum amounts listed, over one-tenth.

To assure enough iron each day, the frequent use of foods important for this mineral needs to be stressed. The better sources of iron include liver, kidney, lean meat, and dry beans. Heart, dark-green leafy vegetables, dried fruit, and molasses also contain appreciable amounts of this nutrient. In the quantities consumed in this country, eggs (yolk) and whole grain, enriched, and restored cereal foods including bread are also valuable sources of iron.

Thiamine.—If average choices are made within food groups, about one-fifth of the adult allowance for thiamine still needs to be furnished. No single food group contributes the major share of this vitamin; however, the meat group supplies the largest portion—about one-third of the day's total.

Thiamine is widely distributed in common foods, though usually in small amounts. Lean pork, however, is outstanding for this nutrient. Among the better sources of thiamine are variety meats, dry beans and peas, and some of the nuts. Whole grain, enriched, or restored cereal products also are important sources. Since there are only a few foods rich in or important for thiamine, it is desirable to use them often.

Riboflavin.—Nearly all the riboflavin recommended for a day is provided for by the kinds and amounts of foods specified in the guide. The milk group furnishes nearly half the daily needs for riboflavin and the meat group accounts for a fourth. The remainder comes about equally from the vegetable-fruit group and the bread-cereals group. The better sources of riboflavin include variety meats—heart, liver, kidney—and milk. Lean meats and many of the dark-green leafy vegetables also furnish worthwhile amounts of this vitamin.

Niacin.—Chart 1 shows that on an average about 10 percent more niacin than is furnished by the food plan is needed to meet the recommended allowance. However, it is possible that the amount of this nutrient already provided for is sufficient. This is because the plan calls for considerable good-quality protein, and the body can change one of the essential amino acids (tryptophan) furnished by this protein into niacin compounds.

Other nutrients.—Although only nine nutrients are discussed in connection with the daily food plan, there are other nutrients present in foods that are important for good nutrition—including known factors and nutrients yet to be identified. Meals that provide recommended amounts of the nine nutrients mentioned probably will be adequate also in these other nutrients.

A varied diet is the best assurance of obtaining all the nutrients essential to good health.

Foods not emphasized in the daily plan—such as fats, oils, sugars, and unenriched refined cereal foods—usually appear in meals in combination with the specified foods and, nutrition-wise, contribute chiefly calories. Hence these foods are not included as groups in the food plan.

Some fat is essential to good nutrition. Fat is an excellent source of calories needed to keep the body functioning, to carry out muscular activities, and to provide warmth. Some fats and oils also furnish essential fatty acids. For example, arachidonic acid is found in animal fats; linoleic and linolenic acids, although present in some animal fats, are found in highest amounts in plant sources. Nuts and unhardened vegetable oils such as corn, cottonseed, and soybean are especially good sources of lineoleic acid. Several fats and oils are carriers of the fat-soluble vitamins. For instance, butter and fortified margarine contain vitamin A, and certain fish oils are rich in both vitamin A and vitamin D. Fat also aids in the absorption of fat-soluble vitamins.

Because fat occurs naturally in many foods, a certain amount will be provided by the foods stressed in the daily plan. For instance, meats, whole milk, cheese made with whole milk, and egg yolk, as well as several other foods, supply fat to the diet. Moreover, food habits in this country are such that fats and oils are added to many other foods in cooking and at the table. Therefore, it is believed that sufficient fat will be provided without special emphasis on this nutrient.

Although sugars are of importance primarily for calories, one of their main contributions to good eating is that they help make meals flavorful and satisfying. This is true also of fats.

Unenriched refined cereals provide some protein and smaller amounts of other nutrients in addition to calories, as well as add variety to meals.

Water is of vital importance to good nutrition. About 7 or 8 cups of fluids are needed each day. More will be necessary in a hot or dry climate or when physical activity is greatly increased.

Basis and use of the daily food plan

This section shows why the different foods and groups of foods stressed in the daily food plan are important to a diet that fully meets recommended allowances and how the plan measures up in providing such a diet.

Food groups.—Each of the four broad food groups listed in the daily food plan—

(1) Milk group—milk, cheese, ice cream;
(2) Meat group—meat, poultry, fish, eggs, dry beans and peas, nuts;
(3) Vegetable-fruit group;
(4) Bread-cereals group—

in the quantities consumed in this country makes a unique contribution to the average diet, in that each provides at least one-fourth the total of two or more nutrients (table 5). Fats, oils, sugars, and sirups are not included as groups in the food plan because in general they are eaten in combination with the other foods mentioned, and their nutritional contribution is mainly in calories.

Evaluation of the food plan.—An appraisal of the daily food plan was made in terms of nutrient values to be expected from its use. Shown in table 6 are the average nutrient contributions of minimum servings from the groups as specified in the plan. These values represent average choices of food items within food groups. Comparison with recommended allowances for an average man or woman shows that additional food is necessary to make up the calorie shortage and to furnish some of the nutrients needed to complete the diet.

Except for calories, iron, and calcium, the level of nutrients provided approximates or exceeds the allowances for an average woman. However, the calorie intake of many women in this country is not much higher than that supplied on an average by the minimum servings specified in the food plan. Because it is difficult to obtain adequate amounts of nutrients at this calorie level without wise food selection, the food plan should be of special value to this group of women. Men generally average a higher calorie intake, so they have a better chance of meeting recommended allowances.

The quantities of foods listed in table 6 represent the *minimum* servings specified in the plan. The amounts of nutrients shown are expected to be supplemented by nutrients from additional servings of these same kinds of foods, as well as by fats and sugars used in cooking or at the table. Whether or not the totals add up to recommended levels for each nutrient depends on the foods chosen to make up the calorie deficit. If the rest of the calories needed come primarily from the foods emphasized in the guide, the remainder of other nutrients will be furnished. If, however, additional calories come largely from fats or sugars, some nutrients are likely to be low.

Largely because of two factors—differences in nutritional needs of individuals and variation in nutritive value of foods—it is practically impossible to devise a general food plan that will be just right for everyone. Foods even within groups differ in nutritive value, so that with day-to-day choices for variety it is not possible to come out with exactly the same amounts of nutrients each day. A food guide for use by a large segment of the population also needs to be flexible enough to allow for regional and seasonal differences in food supplies, for food preferences, and for different food budgets. Hence, a guide such as the daily food plan cannot be expected to guarantee an adequate diet for all.

The food plan in practice.—The specific foods chosen within the general pattern of the daily food plan affect the level of nutrients provided. To give some indication of the results that can be expected, nutrients were calculated for two different combinations of foods selected in accordance with the daily plan (tables 7 and 8). These choices represent only the minimum number of servings suggested from each food group. Items listed in table 7 are commonly used foods; those in table 8 illustrate a wider choice of alternate foods from the food groups.

Both groups of selections provide recommended amounts of vitamins A and C for an average adult; also over 90 percent of the calcium and at least 80 percent of the protein. These nutrients are the ones that are particularly stressed in the food plan, and so it is not surprising that a major part, if not all, of the daily allowances are supplied.

On the other hand, it is less definite that such a large share of daily needs for iron and the B-vitamins will be furnished by the minimum number of servings, because these nutrients are not tied-in with a particular food group. There is considerable variation between the two groups of selections in how well they provide recommended amounts of these essentials. The foods shown in table 7 supply about 60 per-

cent of the iron and niacin, more than 80 percent of the riboflavin, and over 100 percent of the thiamine for an average adult. Those in table 8 provide more than enough iron but only about 70 percent of the thiamine, riboflavin, and niacin. It is evident that foods chosen for the minimum number of servings can be counted on to supply substantial amounts of these nutrients, even though there may be considerable day-to-day variation in the quantities provided.

These examples show that the minimum number of servings specified in the daily food plan go a long way toward providing a nutritionally good diet. They indicate, however, that different choices within the food groups can yield quite different results in terms of nutrients. Moreover, for most people the minimum servings in the food plan make an incomplete diet, in that more food is required for energy needs. These additions, if well chosen, can easily bring the nutrients up to recommended levels; poor choices may add chiefly calories.

Use of food plan for children.—Another illustration of the use of the food plan is given on page 16. Here two menus—one for a 5-year-old child, the other for a teen-age boy 15 years old—have been included to show how the plan can be used with children as well as with adults. Items representing the minimum number of servings suggested in the daily food plan are starred in the menus. Additional foods have been chosen to round out meals and to meet calorie allowances and help supply recommended amounts of other nutrients.

In these menus the food selections are basically the same for the different age children, although the size of the serving and the way the food is prepared may differ. For instance, the 5-year-old has 3 cups of milk, which includes some used in cooking; the older boy, 4½ cups, all as a beverage. These amounts are in line with the quantities of milk suggested in the plan for their age groups. As another example, the teen-ager, with a lunch that could be carried to school, has tuna fish as the filling for his sandwiches, while for the preschool child who eats at home, the smaller serving of tuna fish is creamed.

Because of increased needs for most nutrients, larger servings of some foods as well as additional choices from the four groups are provided for the teen-age boy. An egg is included for

14

breakfast, generous portions of roast beef and vegetables are shown for dinner, and extra servings from the bread-cereal group are used throughout the day. Other examples could be given.

Besides the foods from the groups of the daily food plan, some fats and oils, sugars, and unenriched cereal products are used in these meals to help give satisfaction and to provide food energy and other nutrients. For instance, butter or margarine is included as a spread for bread or to add to vegetables; sugar for the hot cereal and as sweetening for the apple pie and applesauce; mayonnaise for the tuna fish sandwiches for the teen-ager; and unenriched cereal products (flour) might be used by some for the pie crust and cookies.

Choices that represent the minimum number of servings from the food groups suggested in the daily plan, the starred items in the menus, furnish a large share of the nutritional needs of both children. The percentages of recommended dietary allowances [2] provided by these choices are as follows:

Food	5-year-old child	15-year-old boy
Food energy...............	68	55
Protein....................	116	122
Calcium...................	101	107
Iron.......................	76	75
Vitamin A value..........	152	138
Thiamine.................	102	83
Riboflavin................	137	125
Niacin....................	122	121
Ascorbic acid.............	194	131

Except for iron and food energy (calories), the minimum servings listed for the young child furnish more than enough of the nutrients shown. For the 15-year-old boy, thiamine is also short.

The foods added to the minimum servings to complete the meals bring all nine nutrients up to recommended amounts, with generous margins for some. In fact, sufficient vitamin A value is supplied, with carrots as a main source, to meet recommendations for more than 2 days. This is in keeping with the concept presented in the daily food plan that a serving of a dark-green or deep-yellow vegetable at least every other day is adequate to provide the amount of vitamin A value counted on from these foods.

[2] Recommended Dietary Allowances. Food and Nutrition Board. Natl. Res. Council Pub. 302, rev. 1953.

Use of food plans for scoring diets.—Many workers begin nutrition teaching with a group by asking members to keep a record of their meals for one or more days. This is a good way of creating interest on the part of the group. A study of these records shows where emphasis is needed and the food patterns within which adjustments, if any, must be made.

The most obvious and simplest way of appraising the meal record is to count the servings of various types of food and to compare the number with the minimum suggested in some food plan or guide. This will show in a gross way what kinds of food need to be stressed and what dietary shortages might be suspected. For example, if a diet has less than recommended amounts of milk, it is likely to be low in calcium; if dark-green or yellow vegetables are not included frequently, vitamin A may be short; and if citrus fruit or other good sources of vitamin C do not appear in the daily diet, a shortage of vitamin C may be suspected. Other nutrients are not so closely associated with single food groups and their level in diets is not so readily estimated.

The most reliable method of judging dietary adequacy is to calculate from food value tables the nutrients provided by the diet and to compare the results with recommended dietary allowances.

The daily food plan and other food guides.— A food plan or guide to be most useful must be both reliable and simple. Reliability means, of course, that a guide can be depended on to give a nutritionally good diet, while simplicity has to do with how easy it is to use.

To develop a reliable guide, certain basic information must be at hand. This information includes knowledge about dietary shortcomings of individuals, so that in a guide special emphasis can be placed on foods that will supply nutrients found likely to be low. Knowledge of peoples' food habits and of the foods available to them is essential if present food practices are to be modified by a guide only enough to achieve a good diet. A guide will have greater acceptance, if it is in keeping with familiar dietary patterns. Because the daily food plan presented in this publication was intended for use throughout the United States, findings from nationwide food consumption studies were used to furnish this basic information. As a result, the food plan will provide for nutritional needs within the framework of food habits and food supplies of this country.

Reliability of food guides also depends to some extent on choices allowed within food groups. When groups include a wide variety of foods, daily selections may tend to be short in one or more nutrients unless choices are safeguarded. For this reason, certain specifications are made within the broad vegetable-fruit group of the daily food plan. For example, dark-green and deep-yellow vegetables are designated to protect the vitamin A value in diets; the lighter green and pale-yellow vegetables cannot be relied on to contribute enough of this nutrient in ordinary servings, even if used every day.

A final check on the reliability of a food guide is how well the nutrients that can be expected from its use meet the nutritional needs of individuals. For this purpose, as was shown earlier, the National Research Council's recommended dietary allowances were used as a yardstick for evaluating the daily food plan. Other food guides can be tested in the same way to see if they can be counted on to provide for a nutritionally good diet.

Simplicity in a food guide can be achieved in several ways. The number of main food groups in a guide will influence its ease of use. Too many groups are hard to remember, but with too few, there is the likelihood that the day's diet may be short in some essential. The daily food plan has fewer major groups than some other guides, largely because all fruits and vegetables are combined into a single group and because table fats are not listed separately. However, certain choices are qualified within the vegetable-fruit group.

There are several reasons for putting fruits and vegetables together in one group. They can be used interchangeably in meals; as groups they are important primarily for the same nutrients—vitamins A and C; and some of them are valuable sources of both these vitamins. Taking these facts into consideration, it seemed simpler to have fruits and vegetables a single group with special emphasis on those noteworthy for vitamin A value and vitamin C. Greater flexibility for making choices among fruits and vegetables results without sacrificing reliability.

Table fats are not stressed as a special group primarily because their main nutritional contribution is calories, although they add some essential fatty acids and vitamin A. Moreover, their use in meals is quite different from that of other foods, as they are seldom eaten alone. Nearly everyone uses some butter or margarine daily along with other foods, especially breads and vegetables. Hence, elimination of table fats as a group to simplify the food plan is expected to have little effect on the nutritional quality of the diet selected.

Simplicity may also be attained through the kind of names applied to the main food groups of a guide. Some guides have as their chief groups "energy foods," "building foods," and "protective foods." Others stress the major nutrient contribution of foods; to illustrate, the framework might consist of a "protein group," a "B-vitamin group," and so forth. However, it is unlikely that people think about foods in these terms when they market and plan meals. They do not shop for body-building materials or minerals—they buy and serve milk, or meat, or other foods. Therefore, a guide that emphasizes in group titles the kinds of foods that make up the group is probably simpler to use.

It is recognized that there is no one best way to teach wise food selection, as many different combinations of foods can furnish recommended amounts of essential nutrients. In a particular situation, however, one food plan may be more suitable than another. In areas where food customs and food supplies differ considerably from those of the nation as a whole, a food plan other than the one presented here may be preferable, or special guides may need to be developed.

The introduction of a new daily food plan does not mean that the Basic 7 is no longer useful. Many people are well-satisfied with this familiar teaching device. Its continued use is anticipated for as long as it meets their needs. However, it is hoped that both "Essentials of an Adequate Diet" and the daily food plan will be useful tools for those searching for a fresh approach in nutrition education.

Development of a day's meals

Menu for 5-year-old child

Breakfast

*Orange....................	1 medium
*Oatmeal...................	½ cup
Sugar......................	1 teaspoon
*Milk, whole..............	1 cup
*Toast, enriched...........	1 slice
Butter or margarine.......	1 teaspoon

Lunch

*Creamed tuna fish.........	½ cup
*Toast, enriched...........	1 slice
*Carrot strips.............	⅓ medium carrot
Fruited gelatin...........	⅓ cup
Cooky.....................	1 medium
*Milk, whole..............	½ cup

Dinner

*Beef pot roast...........	1½ ounces
*Mashed potatoes..........	¼ cup
*Green peas...............	¼ cup
Celery....................	1 medium stalk
*Bread, enriched..........	1 slice
Butter or margarine.......	1 teaspoon
Applesauce...............	½ cup
*Milk, whole..............	½ cup

Between meal snack

*Milk, whole..............	½ cup
Banana...................	1 medium

Menu for 15-year-old boy

Breakfast

*Orange....................	1 medium
*Oatmeal...................	⅔ cup
Sugar......................	1 teaspoon
*Milk, whole..............	1½ cups
Egg......................	1 egg
Toast, enriched...........	2 slices
Butter or margarine.......	1 teaspoon
Jelly.....................	1 tablespoon

Lunch

*Tuna fish sandwiches.......	1½ sandwiches [1]
*Carrot strips..............	⅔ medium carrot
Tomato wedges...........	1 small tomato
Banana...................	1 medium
Cooky....................	1 medium
*Milk, whole..............	1 cup

Dinner

*Beef pot roast...........	4 ounces
*Mashed potatoes..........	⅔ cup
*Green peas...............	⅔ cup
Celery....................	2 medium stalks
Bread, enriched..........	1 slice
Butter or margarine.......	1 teaspoon
Apple pie................	⅐ of 9-inch pie
*Milk, whole..............	1 cup

Between meal snack

*Milk.....................	1 cup
Apple....................	1 large
Cookies..................	2 medium

*Starred items make up the minimum number of servings suggested from groups of the daily food plan.
[1] Made with 3 slices white enriched bread, 2 ounces tuna fish, 2 tablespoons mayonnaise, 2 leaves lettuce.

Table 5.—Food sources of nutrients: Contribution of 4 food groups to diets of urban families [1]

Food	Food energy	Protein	Calcium	Iron	Vitamin A value	Thiamine	Riboflavin	Niacin	Ascorbic acid
	Pct.	Pct.	Pct.	Pct.	Pct.	Pct.	Pct.	Pct.	Pct.
All foods..........................	100	100	100	100	100	100	100	100	100
Milk, cheese, ice cream............	15	24	64	3	14	10	42	3	4
Meat, poultry, fish, eggs, dry beans and peas, nuts.....	20	40	6	40	14	32	26	49	1
Vegetables and fruits..............	12	10	14	25	61	23	13	18	94
Grain products....................	24	23	14	28	1	32	18	28	(²)
Other foods.......................	29	3	2	4	10	3	1	2	1
Fats and oils......................	17	2	1	2	10	(²)	1	2	0
Sugars, sirups.....................	12	1	1	2	(²)	(²)	(²)	(²)	1

[1] From a survey of food consumption of urban families in the United States, spring 1948.
[2] 0.5 percent or less.

18

Table 6.—Nutrients furnished by daily food plan: Average quantity of nutrients provided by minimum number of servings specified from each food group of the plan and recommended daily allowances for these nutrients

Food	Amount	Food energy	Protein	Calcium	Iron	Vitamin A value	Thiamine [1]	Riboflavin [1]	Niacin [1]	Ascorbic acid [1]
		Cal.	Gm.	Mg.	Mg.	I. U.	Mg.	Mg.	Mg.	Mg.
Milk, cheese, ice cream:										
Milk equivalent [2]	2 cups	390	16.0	514	0.3	870	0.13	0.69	0.4	Trace
Meat, fish, poultry, eggs, dry beans and peas, nuts:										
Meat equivalent [2]	4 ounces, cooked	405	27.1	47	4.6	930	.33	.40	6.0	0
Vegetables and fruits: [3]										
Dark-green and deep-yellow vegetables [4]	1/4 cup	25	1.0	23	.6	2,590	.04	.04	.3	13
Citrus fruits	1/2 cup	55	.9	27	.4	140	.08	.03	.3	53
Other vegetables	1/2 cup	80	2.3	22	.8	80	.07	.05	.9	13
Other fruits	1/2 cup	80	.8	16	.7	560	.04	.05	.4	7
Bread and cereals: [2]										
Whole grain, enriched, restored	4 servings	290	8.8	55	2.1	30	.30	.16	2.5	0
Total		1,255	56.9	704	9.5	5,200	.99	1.42	10.8	86
Recommended dietary allowances: [5]										
Men (U. S. average)		2,700	75.0	800	12.0	5,000	1.40	1.90	14.0	75
Women (U. S. average)		1,900	60.0	800	12.0	4,000	1.00	1.50	10.0	70
Average adult		2,300	68.0	800	12.0	4,500	1.20	1.70	12.0	73

[1] Some cooking losses deducted.
[2] Based on group averages in which nutritive values of individual foods are weighted by proportions in which they were used by U. S. urban families, 1948.
[3] Based on group averages derived from nutritive value of the U. S. per capita food supply, 1952–53.
[4] Values used are a day's share based on 3½ servings weekly—equivalent to a serving every other day.
[5] Allowances for an average U. S. man and woman have been adapted from the National Research Council's recommended dietary allowances (1953) for the 45-year-old man and woman. These allowances were adjusted upwards to conform with the height of the average American of this age, and calories (and related nutrients) were adjusted downwards to conform with activity and environmental temperature typical for this country. Basis for these adjustments are discussed in Applying 1953 Dietary Allowances to U. S. Population Groups. C. LeBovit and H. K. Stiebeling. Jour. Amer. Diet. Assoc. 33: 219–224. 1957. The values shown for an average adult are averages of these adjusted allowances weighted by the proportion of men and women in this country 35 to 54 years of age.